THE CROSS SERIES

CrossFire

*A New Way of Living - **Book 1***

Scott and Sherri Dalton

Hikanos Press

CrossFire
A New Way of Living – Book 1

Book 2 of "The Cross Series" of discipleship and training materials.

Hikanos Press
113 Paramus Ave.
Newark, OH 43055

ISBN 13: 978-1-7361515-1-8

All scriptures used, except where noted, are from The Holy Bible, New International Version®, NIV® Copyright © 2011 by Biblica, Inc.®.

Missio Global School of Ministry

This material is used in conjunction with the Missio Global School of Ministry, a partnership between Missio Global and churches around the world. The School is a valuable one or three-year training program that is based in the local church. It is a proven tool that churches can use to equip their congregation and develop emerging leaders.

For information on hosting a School of Ministry in your church, contact us at: **www.missioglobal.org**.

This material is free upon request in pdf format. It can be reproduced for training purposes only.

Dedication

Since this is our first book we have written together, the dedication must go to our five adult children. We love you more than you can know. You have always been and always will be such a large part of our journey. We can't imagine life without you all.

Acknowledgements

We want to thank and acknowledge the many financial partners of Missio Global who have been so faithful over the past thirteen years, and also to those who have personally supported us even longer. The vision of reaching and equipping the million is being accomplished because of you!

Thanks to Judah Davis and J. Lee Simmons for their input and editing of this book.

The Cross Series

The Cross book series is for Christian growth focusing on discipleship and the initial stages of leadership development. The material is best used in one-on-one mentorship relationships or in small groups. The Cross Series is designed as a growth track that leads to the church-based Missio Global School of Ministry. It can also be used as valuable equipping material for general Christian discipleship.

CrossWalk -First Steps in Your Walk with God
For the newer Christian or for those who want to deepen their walk with God.

CrossFire - A New Way of Living (Books 1 & 2)
Focusing on transforming our values to ones that follow biblical principles, which results in a powerful new way of living!

Project 2T2:2
Making Disciple Makers!

Complete the three books of **The Cross Series** (*CrossWalk* and *CrossFire - Books 1 &2*) and then help guide another person through the books! *Be a disciple maker and help change the world!*

Project 2 Timothy 2:2
And the things you have heard me say in the presence of many witnesses entrust to reliable people who will also be qualified to teach others.

Table of Contents

Table of Contents

Preface

As we journey with Jesus, we find that the things we consider important begin to change. How we spend our time, who we spend it with, and where or on what we spend our money, all begin to change. This happens because our priorities are changing. We are becoming less focused on self. What is important to God now becomes important to us. Things do not change all at once, but as we go through the process of spending time with God and with those who also love him, we see that our previous values (what was important to us) are being replaced with new values.

The two CrossFire study booklets focus on *values that are important in leading a life that is pleasing to God*. These values are not exhaustive – you will encounter others as you continue on your journey. But these values will help you open the door to live a life of purpose where God is exalted and others are honored. It is a new way of living!

Scott and Sherri Dalton
February 2022

How to Use *CrossFire 1*

This book is best used as a discipleship tool between a more mature Christian and another believer or for a small group. The material helps the believer(s) grow in their relationship with God and with a community of believers (the church). Each lesson is to be studied each week over six weeks. Each week includes a short Bible study on the topic of the chapter. The Gospel of Mark and the book of Romans should also be read over the course of the six weeks (a reading guide is provided for each week).

Each person using this book, whether as a growing believer or a more mature believer, should answer the questions before they meet together. It is recommended that the meeting be about one hour. During the meeting, each one should share their own experiences in their journey with Jesus. At the end of each chapter there are applications and next steps to do during the week until the next meeting. "Next Steps" starts with reading a chapter in the Gospel of Mark every day, five days a week, and praying for ten minutes. Other activities are added each week in order to develop spiritual disciplines for growth. You will need a notebook for journaling your thoughts by Lesson 4, but you may use it before that if you wish. Answers for each lesson can be found at the end of this book. Always end each meeting with prayer. Ask the disciple how you can pray for them. Your model of prayer will teach them how to pray.

If you are taking someone through this material, you should read the whole book first to become familiar with its content. Practice the disciplines yourself each week. Make the meetings personal. Share examples and stories from your own life as you lead a young disciple into a deeper relationship with Jesus and with you. Share what God is teaching you as you journey with this person. Discipleship, like salvation, is about relationship – with God and with each other. Enjoy this journey together as you both come to know God at a deeper level.

LESSON 1

Becoming a Disciple

"Follow Me"

Jesus wants us to be with him! Jesus approached those whom he was calling to be his disciples with those simple yet profound words, "Follow me." He was not speaking figuratively, but was literally calling them to leave everything and follow him. It was a serious life changing commitment. It still is today.

To be a disciple is to be a student, to learn from a master. What was unusual about Jesus was that he approached the people he was calling to be his students. In that era, it was the student that pursued a master for training. But Jesus, the master, took the initiative to call his students, chosen from among people that no one had ever chosen before. He has chosen you, too, and wants you to follow near to him because he wants to show you a new way of living!

> *[14]He appointed twelve that they might **be with him** and that he might **send them out** to preach[15] and to have **authority** to drive out demons.* (Mark 3:14-15)

As we spend time with Jesus our lives are transformed to be more like his. We are empowered to do the works that he did. In fact, Jesus said we would do even greater things than he did (John 14:12)! As you grow in your spiritual walk with Jesus, he will give you greater spiritual authority. Jesus wants to "send you out" with this authority so that you can be a blessing to others by demonstrating his love and power to them.

> *[24]The student is not above the teacher, nor a servant above his master. [25]It is enough for students to be like their teachers, and servants like their masters.* (Matthew 10:24-25)

As a student, your goal is to become like the teacher. Jesus wants you to be like him! Becoming like Jesus is not about "knowing" a lot of Bible information; it's about "knowing" Jesus personally. The more time you spend and devote to Jesus, you will know him more and become more like him. Answer his call of "follow me" every day.

Take My Yoke Upon You

Becoming a disciple of Jesus is like an apprenticeship. It is a learning relationship. It does take discipline on our part to be a disciple; discipline is the root word of disciple. However, the objective of discipleship is not to be burdensome, but to give us rest. Jesus gave us a powerful image of this when he said,

> [28]*Come to me, all you who are weary and burdened, and I will give you rest.* [29]***Take my yoke upon you and learn from me****, for I am gentle and humble in heart, and you will find rest for your souls.* [30]*For **my yoke is easy and my burden is light***. (Matthew 11:28-30)

A yoke is an instrument of hard work that was used (and in some places still is used) with farm animals to plow a field or pull a heavy cart. It is the thing that goes around the animal's neck and is attached to the plow or cart. So why would Jesus call people to his rest by speaking about an instrument of hard work? Why would Jesus use a yoke to describe life in relationship with him?

When farmers are training young oxen to plow a field, the young ox always wants to wander off. They are not comfortable with the yoke and do not understand this new activity of plowing a field. So the farmer always puts the young ox in one yoke with an experienced ox in the other yoke (the yokes are attached on the same beam of wood). The experienced ox trains the young ox to stay on the right path so the field is plowed. And the young ox probably gives some new energy to the experienced one!

Jesus takes this illustration even further by saying his yoke is easy and his burden is light. How can the burden of his yoke be light? It is because he is bearing most of the burden of the heavy load! We just need to stay near him in the yoke and he does most of the work. This is how we learn from him. *The only way we can learn from Jesus is by taking his yoke upon us.*

Jesus will use his disciples here and now (the more experienced oxen) to help train newer disciples. As you complete this book, someone should be accompanying you to help you grow in your spiritual journey with Jesus. We call this person a guide. They are with you to give support, encouragement, and at times some help with direction. Their role is to always point you toward Jesus. Your guide is not perfect like Jesus, so you will need to give them grace at times. They are farther along in their journey with Jesus and care for you very much. Together you can "plow a lot of fields" for the Kingdom!

A LOOK AT THE WORD

1. Read Mark 3:14-15.
   Why did Jesus appoint the 12 disciples? _____

   _____

   _____

   Why is it important for you to be with Jesus? _____

   _____

   How can you do that? _____

   _____

   _____

   _____

2. Read Matthew 10:24-25.
   What is the goal of a student? _____

   _____

   Besides Jesus, can you name any teachers in your life that you want to be like? _____

   _____

3. Read Matthew 11:28-30.
   What is a yoke? _____

   _____

Why is the yoke of Jesus easy and his burden light? _____

_____

_____

If you feel like the yoke of Jesus is heavy, why might that be?

_____

_____

_____

4. Read John 14:12-14.
    Why will we be able to do greater things than Jesus? _____

    _____

    _____

    How can we do that? _____

    _____

5. Read Matthew 28:18-20, which is often referred to as the Great
    Commission. The main verb in this Scripture is not "go" but "make
    disciples." The other verbs – go, baptize, and teach – tell us how
    we are to make disciples.
    According to this Scripture what was Jesus' priority? Why?

    _____

    _____

    Who is someone who can teach you? _____

    _____

    Who is someone you can teach? _____

    _____

APPLICATION

Jesus' final words in Matthew 28:18-20 make it clear that making
disciples was to be a priority and main focus for his followers. He not
only wants all his followers to be disciples and become spiritually
mature, he also wants them to disciple others to maturity. *This is to*

be the mission of every Christian and every church until Jesus returns.

During this next week, do the "Next Steps" listed below as you journey on the road to maturity. If someone is taking you through this study, you already have identified someone who can teach you. If not, find someone who has been following Jesus longer than you and see if they can journey alongside you. Finally, pray and identify someone who you can begin a discipleship journey with, where you teach them what you have learned about Jesus and the kingdom of God. You could take them through *CrossWalk: First Steps in Your Walk with God* as a starting point.

NEXT STEPS

Bible reading this week

Mark 1-5. Begin to read the Gospel of Mark. Try to read one chapter a day for five days each week. Mark has sixteen chapters so you will finish the book in three weeks by reading one extra chapter the last week. Use the weekend to make up any chapters you may have missed. Pay attention to whom Jesus speaks and what he teaches. What are the responses of the different people? Use the following "OIA" questions as you think about and meditate on what you read:

> **Observation** - What does it *say*? (Answer questions like: Who is involved in the story? What is happening? Where is the story or teaching taking place: in a city, by a lake, in the desert? What are people thinking or feeling? Is Jesus teaching through a parable, using Scriptures, or answering a question someone asked? Is he teaching his 12 disciples, multitudes, religious leaders? What kind of miracles occur and why?)

> **Interpretation** - What does it *mean*? (Answer questions like: How were these observations interpreted by Jesus, people present, or the readers at that time? Remember this rule of interpretation – Scripture cannot mean to us today what it never meant to people in the time period in which it was written.)

> **Application** - What does it mean *for me*? (Answer questions like: How can you apply this to your life, your circumstances, or

to others?) Write down what you learn from God or about God.

Prayer

Pray for 10 minutes a day this week. Simply talk to God like you would a close friend. Thank him for your new life, ask him to lead you through the day, pray for your needs, and ask him to bless the people who are close to you.

LESSON 2

Making Jesus Lord

Declare With Your Mouth

It is a bold position to declare Jesus as your Lord. Many Christians have been killed through the ages for making such a claim, and that still happens today. You have been rescued from the dominion of darkness (Satan's worldly kingdom) and have been brought into the Kingdom of the son God loves, with King Jesus on the throne (Colossians 1:13). You live in a world where these two kingdoms are constantly in conflict. You will find yourself at times right in the crossfire. But you can be confident because you are a citizen in the Kingdom that has already won the war!

> *⁹If you declare with your mouth, "Jesus is Lord," and believe in your heart that God raised him from the dead, you will be saved. ¹⁰For it is with your heart that you believe and are justified, and it is with your mouth that you profess your faith and are saved.* (Romans 10:9-10)

When you gave your life to Christ you may have actually prayed Romans 10:9-10. In order to receive God's salvation and have your sins forgiven, you must believe in your heart that Jesus is alive, AND declare with your mouth that "Jesus is Lord." It is that declaration of the lordship of Jesus in your life that marks the moment of your salvation. As a Christian you must follow Jesus as your Lord. That means he is the master of your life, and that is a good thing because he has only good things in store for you!

You may hear at some point that some people seem to treat Jesus as only their Savior but not their Lord. In truth there is no such thing as accepting Jesus as your Savior but not as your Lord. The very act of salvation requires you to declare Jesus as your Lord. Salvation (Christ as your Savior) is simply the first step in a lifelong journey of Jesus being the Lord of your life.

Carry Your Cross

Jesus made some very strong statements about what it means to be his disciple. It sounds very much like Jesus has to be Lord of every area of your life. Basically you need to die to your selfish sinful desires and pursue a righteous life with Jesus. Here is what Jesus said.

> [23]*Then he said to them all: "Whoever wants to be my disciple must **deny themselves and take up their cross daily and follow me.** [24]For whoever wants to save their life will lose it, but whoever loses their life for me will save it. [25]What good is it for someone to gain the whole world, and yet lose or forfeit their very self?"* (Luke 9:23-25)

What happens on a cross is not pleasant. Death happens on a cross. But Jesus already died in your place on his cross to pay the penalty for your sins. The cross that we need to pick up daily now means death to our selfish and sinful desires. That is what it means to "deny yourself." It means to follow Jesus every day and seek to live your life following his ways. His ways are always much better than our ways!

Later in Luke, it is recorded that Jesus again said that in order to be his disciple a person must carry his own cross (Luke 14:27). He concluded by saying in Luke 14:33, "In the same way, those of you who do not give up everything you have cannot be my disciples." Each of us must "count the cost" in following Jesus. It means we must be willing to give up anything for him. It does not mean that Jesus is going to take everything good from us. Just the opposite. He wants us to give up the bad or unhealthy things so that he can give us his best. It means we must surrender to him and truly make Jesus our Lord.

Idols of the Heart

Idolatry sounds like something that happened in ancient times, but it is very much practiced today, although sometimes in a subtler manner. *If anything is more important to you than Jesus, that thing is an idol (or lord) in your life.* An idol could even be a person or your career, not just an object. Let's look at an actual occurrence that Jesus encountered as seen in the Gospel of Mark.

*¹⁷As Jesus started on his way, a man ran up to him and fell on his knees before him. "Good teacher," he asked, "**what must I do** to inherit eternal life?" ¹⁸"Why do you call me good?" Jesus answered. "No one is good—except God alone. ¹⁹You know the commandments: 'You shall not murder, you shall not commit adultery, you shall not steal, you shall not give false testimony, you shall not defraud, honor your father and mother.'" ²⁰"Teacher," he declared, "all these I have kept since I was a boy." ²¹Jesus looked at him and loved him. "One thing you lack," he said. "Go, sell everything you have and give to the poor, and you will have treasure in heaven. Then come, follow me." ²²At this the man's face fell. He went away sad, because he had great wealth.* (Mark 10:17-22)

Notice that this man ran up to Jesus and knelt before him, earnestly inquiring about how he could receive eternal life. But Jesus noticed the man had asked, "What must I do?" So Jesus tested him by telling him to observe the six commandments that address our external actions as opposed to what we set our heart on. The man replied with confidence that he had kept those commands since his youth. Then Jesus identified the idol in the man's life by telling him to sell and give away all his possessions then come and follow him. The man walked away sad, and Jesus did not go after him. At that moment, at least, the man's wealth was more important than following Jesus. His wealth was an idol to him.

Jesus very rarely asks his followers to do things like quit their jobs, sell everything, and move to another country (although he did ask our family to do that!). He wants you to not cling to or set your affections on the things of this world. God wants to give you abundant provision, but the provision is to fulfill his purpose in your life and still have enough left over for you to bless others. *Lordship is an attitude of the heart first, then an action.* It is not just outward sacrifice, but a heart issue (1 Corinthians 13:3). Jesus wants to be Lord of your heart.

Although God is patient with you and does not expect instant transformation in your life, he does expect you to *be willing* to change when he tells you. If there is a sin that you are unwilling to quit, a thing you could never part with, a person whose opinion matters more than God's to you, a person you can never forgive, or even a place you could never move from or to, then that is a sign that you have an idol in your life. Ask God to search your heart, confess it to him and to your guide, and thank God for all the good things that he has for you. Jesus is a wonderful Lord!

A LOOK AT THE WORD

1. Read Romans 10:9-10.
    What two things must you do to be saved? _____
    _____
    _____

    Why must you do both? Have you done this? _____
    _____
    _____
    _____

2. Read Luke 9:23-25.
    What does Jesus say you must do to be his disciple?
    _____
    _____

    What does that mean? _____
    _____
    _____

    Why did he say you must do that? _____
    _____
    _____

3. Read Luke 14:27 and 33.
    What must you do to be a disciple of Jesus? _____

_____

_____

What might God be asking you to give up? _____

_____

_____

4. Read Mark 10:17-22.
    What did the man ask Jesus? _____

    _____

    Did he keep the commandments listed by Jesus? _____

    What did Jesus say he also needed to do? _____

    _____

    How did the man respond and why? _____

    _____

    Can you give up everything and everyone, or is there something
    or someone that is difficult for you to give up? If there is, write it
    below and talk about it with your guide. _____

    _____

    _____

    _____

5. Read 1 Corinthians 13:3.
    Is giving to the poor or living in hardship necessarily evidence that
    Jesus is Lord of your heart? Why or not?

    _____

    _____

    _____

    _____

APPLICATION

Making Jesus Lord of your life means you show your love for
him by putting him first. This is reflected in your lifestyle, relation-

ships, and decisions. It certainly means making some decisions that will not be very popular with people who are not following Jesus. Making Jesus Lord means you need to die to your selfish and hurtful desires while you are pursuing a new and wonderful life in Jesus!

Being a disciple of Jesus means you love him and put him first before everyone and everything. Is there anything in your life that might be more important than following Jesus? As you do "Next Steps," write these down and pray for God to help you love Jesus more. He is able to change your heart if you truly desire to place him first.

NEXT STEPS

Bible reading this week

Mark 6-10. Continue to read the Gospel of Mark. Try to read one chapter a day for five days each week. Use the weekend to make up any chapters you may have missed. Pay attention to whom Jesus speaks and what he teaches. What are the responses of the different people? Use the "OIA" questions (Observation, Interpretation, and Application, see Lesson 1 "Next Steps") as you think about and meditate on what you read.

Prayer

Pray for 10 minutes a day this week. Simply talk to God like you would a close friend. Thank him for your new life, ask him to lead you through the day, pray for your needs, and ask him to bless the people you are close to.

Obedience

Sacrifice: Make a list of things you need to give up to better serve and love Jesus.

LESSON 3

Obedience
The Law vs. The Heart

Obeying the "Rules"

The most common misconception of Christianity is that it is simply a set of rules that we must follow or else God will be upset with us. If you come from a religious culture you have probably experienced the fear of "breaking the rules" and being worried that God will punish you. To be very clear, that is NOT God's heart toward you at all.

The rules, or commands, that God gives to us are like a fence near a dangerous cliff. They are for our protection. Imagine parents allowing their small child to play in a dangerous area without a protective fence. God wants to protect you, in the same way, from emotional and even physical harm. He wants you to have healthy relationships and for you to know his purpose for your life. Remember, God is always good and wants the best for you!

As we grow in our maturity in Christ we are more sensitive to the leading of the Holy Spirit and are better able to make wise decisions. Even so, we always need to be cautious of putting ourselves in a situation that could lead to sin. Plus, we must remember that our adversary, the evil one, does plan schemes against us. Jesus wants to protect us.

The "Law of Christ" is a Heart Issue

It is critical to understand that obedience to God is much deeper than simply following "an ancient set of rules." Our actions are very important, but our actions and words flow out from our heart. *Obedience is a heart issue.* You could be doing and saying all the "right things," but your heart could be very far from God. When you are following the rules but not truly surrendering your heart to God, it is called "legalism" or a "religious spirit." It is an outward obligation, not an inward faith of the heart.

Jesus is most concerned about your heart. If your heart is right, the right actions will follow. The "Law of Christ" is focused on the heart. He made this very clear in what is called his Sermon on the Mount. Jesus was teaching about the Law of Moses given to the Israelites, but he completely took it to another level! Here are a couple excerpts from this preaching in Matthew 5:

> *21 You have heard that it was said to the people long ago, "You shall not murder, and anyone who murders will be subject to judgment." 22 But I tell you that anyone who is angry with a brother or sister will be subject to judgment.*
> *27 You have heard that it was said, **"You shall not commit adultery." 28 But I tell you that anyone who looks at a woman lustfully has already committed adultery with her in his heart.***

The crowd was accustomed to hearing about the religious laws, what they could do and not do according to the Law. But Jesus goes much deeper, literally to the heart of the sin problem. He was telling them that sin begins in the heart and that God would hold them responsible for the sin of their heart, not just their outward actions. This is not about temptation. We are all tempted (even Jesus was) but can overcome it and not sin. But you know when you are looking at a woman (or a man) lustfully, and God does too. He calls it sin.

You are probably thinking, "What a minute, Jesus. That is pretty radical!" You are correct; Jesus is radical about sin because it is so destructive and causes spiritual death. He died and rose again so that you can be free from sin and live the abundant life he has for you!

It's About Love Not Law

Whether you sin or not does not change God's love for you. God does not love you less when you sin, and he does not love you more when you don't. But God's love for you is not the issue. *Your love for him is the issue.* Jesus told his disciples,

If you love me, keep my commands. (John 14:15)

If we truly love Jesus we will not want to sin. Sin, your sin, sent Jesus to the cross. He went to the cross willingly to take the punishment you deserve. It is the heart of a disciple of Jesus to willingly follow him and leave that ugly sin behind. *Obedience is not about following the Law or religious rules; it's about following and loving Jesus.*

Are You Following the Law Instead of Jesus?

The truth is that many Christians are still trying to follow the Law rather than follow Jesus. They are still living in an "Old Testament mentality" (follow the rules) rather than the New Covenant we have in Christ (be near to God). Do not fall into this trap. Jesus has a new way of living for you!

How can you know if your heart is right before God? How can you be sure that you are following the heart of Jesus and not just following rules? Here is the answer. If you ask, "Is it permitted for Christians to do (fill in the blank)" then you are following the Law. Yes, there are lists of common sins in the Bible that are always sin (do not murder, etc.). Most people and cultures recognize those actions as sin. But what about the everyday situations that you encounter?

Following the Law always looks for the limit of what is "permitted" by the Law. You try to go "right to the edge of sin" but still stay in the area that is permitted. That is totally following the Law! *If you are following Jesus, you will try to stay as far as possible from sin to be near him.*

The question you should ask yourself when you are faced with a decision is not "Is this *permitted* for Christians?" The right question to ask is "Is this *pleasing* to God?" You should be willing to surrender to God, not assert your "rights" to certain activities or things. Follow Jesus, love him, and obey him!

A LOOK AT THE WORD

1. Read Matthew 5:21-22.
   In addition to killing someone, what does Jesus consider murder?

   _____

   _____

   Both were subject to what? _____

   Read Matthew 5:27-28.
   What else does Jesus consider adultery? Why? _____

   _____

   _____

2. Read John 14:15.
   How do you show your love for Jesus? _____

   _____

   _____

3. Read John 14:23-24.
   How can you know who loves Jesus and who does not? _____

   _____

   _____

   What is the reward for obedience? _____

   _____

   _____

4. Read Luke 11:28.
   Who did Jesus say are blessed? _____

   _____

   How can you be blessed? _____

   _____

5. Read 2 John 1:6
   How can you walk in love? _____

   _____

APPLICATION

In Romans 6:16 Paul says, "Don't you know that when you offer yourselves to someone as obedient slaves, you are slaves of the one you obey – whether you are slaves to sin, which leads to death, or to obedience, which leads to righteousness?" We are all slaves to who or what we obey. If we obey sin, it leads to death; if we obey Jesus and his teachings, it leads to righteousness and eternal life.

Together read the following Scriptures which include a list of common sins: 1 Corinthians 6:9-10; Galatians 5:19-21; Ephesians 5:3-6. You may find some of the same sins in each list, but note these lists are not exhaustive. Discuss the different sins and why God would consider them sinful. Do you need to confess any of the sins listed?

Determine this week to show your love for Jesus by obeying him, even when it is hard or causes people to think or speak against you. Also, be sure to obey your parents if you still live in their home, teachers if you are in school, and any supervisor at work. God assures a blessing if you do. Write about your experiences below in Next Steps.

NEXT STEPS

Bible reading this week

Mark 11-16. Finish reading Mark this week. Remember you will need to read an extra chapter. Use the weekend to read the extra chapter or to make up any chapters you may have missed. Pay attention to whom Jesus speaks and what he teaches. What are the responses of the different people? Use the "OIA" questions (Observation, Interpretation, and Application, see Lesson 1 "Next Steps") as you think about and meditate on what you read.

Prayer

Pray for 10 minutes a day this week. Simply talk to God like you would a close friend. Thank him for your new life, ask him to lead you through the day, pray for your needs, and ask him to bless the people you are close to.

Obedience

Write briefly about a situation that occurred this week in which you chose to obey Jesus even though it was difficult. How did you feel after you obeyed or overcame temptation?

In what ways can you obey Jesus this week. List them below.

Is there anyone to whom you need to obey or submit? List them below.

LESSON 4

Sanctification
Becoming More Like Jesus

Sanctification is one of those long religious sounding words. It is the process of becoming holy, or pursuing a righteous lifestyle without sin. Actually, we have already talked about it before. It is simply becoming more like Jesus. Although the definition is simple, it does not sound so simple to become more like Jesus! But you need to understand the following vital truth before we learn more about sanctification.

Perfect Yet Being Made Holy

*For by one sacrifice (the death of Jesus) he **has made perfect** forever those who are **being made holy**.* (Hebrews 10:14 - parenthesis added)

This is an incredible verse and you need to grasp this truth! When you surrendered to Jesus and made him Lord of your life, your sins were completely forgiven because Jesus paid the penalty for them, taking your punishment on the cross. At that moment, in God's eyes, you were "made perfect" in the sense that God sees no sin in you! Your sins have been cast as far as the east is from the west (Psalm 103:12)! You are truly sinless in his sight. This part of the verse speaks about the *moment* of salvation. It happens in an instant and the sin that caused the separation between you and God is completely removed. Thank you Jesus!

The second half of the verse speaks about the *process* of sanctification. As a Christian, you are free from the *penalty* and even the *power* of sin. But in life on this fallen earth, you are not yet free from the *presence* of sin. You are still capable of falling into a sin. God's forgiveness is always there. Repent and turn to him quickly and you will receive his forgiveness and restoration (1 John 1:9). It is a process to become more and more like Jesus. But be assured this is God's plan for you, and by the power of the Holy Spirit and your determination, you can do it! When you submit to God in this manner you can be assured that you are "being made holy." God is so Good!

Slave to Righteousness or Slave to Sin

The Apostle Paul, writing in the book of Romans, makes a very strong declaration when he says we are all slaves to the one we obey (Romans 6:16). Another way of thinking about this is whatever we serve, whether it is a person, thing, or even a thought, it is our master. Take a few minutes right now to pause from this study, and **please read all of chapter 6 of Romans in your Bible.** It will help you understand this concept much better.

> [19b]*Just as you used to offer yourselves as **slaves to impurity and to ever-increasing wickedness**, so now offer yourselves as **slaves to righteousness** leading to holiness (sanctification). [20]When you were **slaves to sin**, you were free from the control of righteousness. [21]What benefit did you reap at that time from the things you are now ashamed of? Those things result in **death!** [22]But now that you have been **set free from sin** and have become **slaves of God**, the benefit you reap leads to holiness (sanctification), and the result is **eternal life**.* (Romans 6:19b-22 - words in parenthesis added for clarification)

This portion of Romans 6 reveals a couple important truths. First, in the eyes of God, we are all slaves to one of two things – righteousness or sin. Someone may say, "Hey, I do what I want. I'm not a slave to anything!" The truth is if you are trying to do your "own thing" without God, you are actually a slave to impurity, wickedness, and sin with the result being "death."

Second, you cannot serve both righteousness and sin at the same time. Verse 22 says when you are "set free from sin" you are now a "slave of God." That may sound harsh, but you are also a son or daughter of Father God, a co-heir with Jesus of a great inheritance, and a citizen of the Kingdom of God with all its benefits! What Paul is trying to emphasize in this passage is that to whatever you submit or offer yourself, you are a slave of that thing. So submit yourself to God, not sin. The result of your choice leads to eternal life or death.

Consecrate Yourselves to God

Many times in the Bible the people of God were called to consecrate themselves, especially before a religious event or an important activity like a battle. This is a very similar concept to sanctification. It is easy to fall into the trap that this means simply to "stop sinning" or to separate yourself from sin. In truth, consecration means to draw near to God. This means you need to separate yourself from opportunities to sin, but the emphasis is on desiring to be close to God. Remember from Lesson 3, we said that if you are following Jesus you will want to stay far from sin and be near to him. Staying near to Jesus is the key. If you do, even thinking about sin happens less and less frequently.

> [1]*Therefore, since we are surrounded by such a great cloud of witnesses, let us **throw off everything that hinders** and **the sin that so easily entangles**. And let us run with perseverance the race marked out for us,* [2]*fixing our eyes on Jesus, the pioneer (author) and perfecter of faith.* (Hebrews 12:1-2a)

These New Testament verses from the book of Hebrews illustrate this truth. You are in a new race now – the race to fulfill God's purpose in your life! Do you want to carry heavy weights or be entangled by chains of sin in this race? Of course not! You want to run the best way you can. Other followers of Christ are cheering you onward. Run with perseverance, keeping your eyes on Jesus (staying near to him). Jesus began this work in your heart, and you can trust him to make your faith "perfect." Along the journey of this race you will become more and more like Jesus. One day you will see him face to face as he waits for you at the finish line!

A LOOK AT THE WORD

1. Read Hebrews 10:14.
    How can we be "perfect" now while still being "made holy?"

    _____

    _____

    _____

    _____

    _____

2. Read Romans 6:19b-22.
    To what did you offer yourself before walking with Jesus?

    _____

    When you were a slave to sin, from what were you free?

    _____

    What was the result? _____

    Now to whom are you a slave? _____

    What are you set free from? _____

    What is the result? _____

3. Read Hebrews 12:1-2a.
    What are you to throw off? _____

    _____

    Then what are you to do? How? _____

    _____

    How is Jesus described in these verses? _____

    _____

    What is the race marked out for you personally now? Do you have
    a sense of God's purpose for your life? _____

    _____

    _____

    _____

4. Read 1 Timothy 4:7-8.
   What is the value of physical training? _____

   _____

   Why does training yourself to be godly have more value?

   _____

   _____

   What practical steps can you take to train yourself to be godly?

   _____

   _____

   _____

   _____

APPLICATION

Discuss with your guide ways you can train yourself to be godly. (Remember that physical training is of "some value," so taking better care of yourself physically may be included.) Part of that training includes confessing sins, asking forgiveness, and forgiving others. You may want to review the Scriptures about sin from last week: 1 Corinthians 6:9-10; Galatians 5:19-21. Why should we acknowledge what the Bible says is sinful, rather than what the world says is sinful? Is there any sin you need to confess? Is there anyone you need to ask forgiveness of or who you need to forgive? Do it now with your guide so that you can get into a habit of confessing and forgiving.

If you are struggling with reading your Bible and praying daily, talk to your guide and have him/her pray for you. It is said that it takes 30 days to create a habit. With your guide, set a time for your devotional each day this week. Set a goal that for the next 30 days you will not go to bed at night until you take the time to read and pray, if you had not done so earlier in the day.

NEXT STEPS

Bible reading this week

Romans 1-5. Begin to read Romans. Try to read one chapter a day for five days each week, using the weekend to make up any chapters you may have missed. Romans has sixteen chapters so you should finish Romans in three weeks, reading six chapters the last week, which will be after Lesson 6 of this booklet. Romans is a letter written by the apostle Paul to the church in Rome. The focus is the righteousness of God and how God's grace is more powerful than sin. You can still use the basic "OIA" questions as you read Romans.

> *Observation* - What does it *say?*
>
> *Interpretation* - What does it *mean?*
>
> *Application* - What does it mean *for me?*
> (Write down what you learn from God or about God.)

Prayer

Pray for 10 minutes a day this week. Simply talk to God like you would a close friend. Thank him for your new life, ask him to lead you through the day, pray for your needs, and ask him to bless the people you are close to.

Obedience

This week you will work on training yourself to be godly. Write in your journal when you will schedule your devotional time. Write what you will do this week as part of your self-training.

LESSON 5

Forgiveness
Receiving and Giving

You Are Forgiven!

Every day you can rejoice and thank God that your sins are completely forgiven when you confess them to Jesus! Jesus' death on the cross was the complete work for your forgiveness for all time. Declare the following verses that your sin is forgiven, covered, and will never count against you.

> *7Blessed are those whose transgressions(sins) are **forgiven**, whose sins are **covered**.*
> *8Blessed is the one whose sin the Lord will **never count against them**.* (Romans 4:7-8, a quotation from Psalm 32:1-2)

If you are new in your journey with Jesus, some of your friends and family may question your commitment to God. They may say things like, "How can you follow Jesus after all the bad things you have done?" Certainly Satan, your adversary, will accuse you and try to discourage you. But you can confidently say to them all that you have been forgiven and are clean! The Lord will never count your sin against you.

You will undoubtedly encounter moments when you think you have done something that God simply cannot forgive. You may sin again in an area of struggle in your life. You can be free from that sin, but the first thing you must remember is that God is always ready to forgive and restore you. Do not ever give in to the lie that God will not forgive you! He has promised to forgive you, as seen in this well-known verse:

> *If we confess our sins, he is **faithful and just** and will **forgive us** our sins and purify us from all unrighteousness.* (1 John 1:9)

If you do sin, confess it quickly to the Lord. God is faithful to forgive and purify you from unrighteousness. Then seek to be ever nearer to Jesus like we learned in the previous lesson of sanctification. (If you feel it would be helpful, confess it to a trusted friend or your guide in this study so that they can stand with you in prayer.)

Forgive Seventy Times Seven

Forgiveness is a major characteristic of God. If we are to be like him, we need to learn to forgive others. Just like we have been forgiven by God, we need to be quick to forgive others who have sinned against us. Sometimes we may get tired of being offended or hurt by someone. Peter asked Jesus how many times we should forgive someone. Jesus answered Peter and told a parable. **Please read the entire parable in Matthew 18:21-35**, as only a part of it is quoted below.

> *21 Then Peter came to Jesus and asked, "Lord, how many times shall I forgive my brother or sister who sins against me? Up to seven times?" 22 Jesus answered, "I tell you, not seven times, but seventy times seven."* (Matthew 18:21-22)

> *32 Then the master called the servant in. "You wicked servant," he said, "I canceled all that debt of yours because you begged me to. 33 Shouldn't you have had mercy on your fellow servant just as I had on you?" 34 In anger his master handed him over to the jailers to be tortured, until he should pay back all he owed.*

> *35 This is how my heavenly Father will treat each of you unless you forgive your brother or sister* **from your heart**. (Matthew 18:32-35)

In the parable, the wicked servant who was forgiven much by the master would not forgive someone who owed him much less. The master's response was severe. Not forgiving someone from your heart (sincere forgiveness) has serious consequences. Forgiveness is not a feeling; you must *choose* to forgive. But it is more than a choice because forgiveness is actually an *obligation* on our part if we want God to forgive us. Jesus directly said if you do not forgive the sin of others, then God will not forgive your sins (Matthew 6:15).

The Chains of Unforgiveness

There is perhaps no greater stronghold or barrier in your spiritual growth than unforgiveness. It is like a chain that binds your heart. There is a heavy weight attached to that chain and it will drag you down into bitterness and even rage. Unforgiveness will destroy your relationships with other people (not just the one who sinned against you) and certainly your relationship with God.

¹²And forgive us our debts (sins), as we also have forgiven our debtors (those who sin against us).
¹³And lead us not into temptation, but deliver us from the evil one.
*¹⁴For **if you forgive other people when they sin against you,** your heavenly Father will also forgive you. ¹⁵But if you do not forgive others their sins, your Father will not forgive your sins.* (Matthew 6:12-15 - text in parentheses and bolded words added for clarity)

Forgiving someone else is not dependent upon them asking you for forgiveness. Verse 14 does not say, "If you forgive someone **when they ask** for forgiveness." When you hold unforgiveness toward someone else, you may think you are punishing them by not speaking to them, etc. But the opposite is true! You are bound by the chains of unforgiveness and cannot move past the offense. You know this is true because you can never seem to escape the bitterness and hurt.

It is not without purpose that verse 13 is in between verses talking about forgiveness. The evil one loves to separate relationships and unforgiveness is one of his greatest weapons. *Forgiveness is a decision, not a feeling.* Repent of not forgiving others. Ask God to help you forgive. Speak the words out loud, forgive those who have hurt you, ask God to bless them, release them to God, and be released yourself. Be free from the chains!

A LOOK AT THE WORD

1. Read 1 John 1:9.
    When we confess our sins what is God always faithful and just to do?

    _____

    _____

2. Read Ephesians 1:7-8.
    What does redemption mean? _____

    _____

    We have redemption and forgiveness of sins according to what?

    _____

    _____

    How much of God's grace are we given (what does lavish mean)?

    _____

    _____

    _____

3. Read Matthew 18:21-35.
    How many times must we forgive someone who sins against us (verse 22)? _____

    Jesus tells a parable about two men who owe money. How much does the first man owe (vs. 24)? _____

    What was to be done to pay the debt (vs. 25)? _____

    _____

    When the servant asked for mercy what did the master do (vs. 27)? _____

    How much did the second man owe his fellow servant (vs. 28)?

    _____

    When the second man asked for mercy what did his fellow servant do (vs. 30)? _____

    _____

Had the servant received his money would it have been enough to pay off his debt to the master? _____

What did the master call the servant who refused to forgive the debt (vs. 32)? What did he do with the servant and why (verses 33-34)? _____

_____

_____

How big is the debt you owe to Jesus? What is the lesson Jesus was teaching (vs. 35)? _____

_____

_____

_____

4.   Read Matthew 6:14-15.

Why is it important to forgive others when they sin against you?

_____

_____

_____

How will forgiving others deliver us from the evil one? _____

_____

_____

_____

APPLICATION

An important concept to understand in 1 John 1:9 is that God is not only faithful to forgive us when we repent, but he is also just to forgive us. You may understand that he is faithful to forgive, but what does his justice have to do with forgiving us? The answer is that God has a Kingdom and his Kingdom has laws. One of God's laws is "The wages of sin is death" (Romans 6:23a). This means that the payment (wage) for those who sin is they will die. In the Old Testament, God instituted a law that he would forgive sin with a blood sacrifice of an animal. Jesus replaced once and for all time the animal sacrifices with his own death on the cross. All those who believe and accept his death as payment for their sin are now forgiven. Because Jesus has now paid the price for our sin, *justice demands that we be forgiven* and cleansed from all unrighteousness when we repent and confess our sin to God. The promise of eternal life is also important because even though our earthly bodies will die, we will live eternally with God and one day we will receive a heavenly body like Jesus has now. Write your answers in your journal for the questions below in Next Steps.

NEXT STEPS

Bible reading this week

Romans 6-10. Continue to read Romans. Try to read one chapter a day for five days each week, using the weekend to make up any chapters you may have missed. Romans has 16 chapters so you should finish Romans in three weeks, reading six chapters the last week, which will be after Lesson 6 of this booklet. Romans is a letter written by the apostle Paul to the church in Rome. The focus is the righteousness of God and how God's grace is more powerful than sin. You can still use the questions of Observation, Interpretation, Application (see Lesson 4) as you read Romans.

Prayer

Pray for 10 minutes a day this week. Simply talk to God like you would a close friend. Thank him for your new life, ask him to lead you through the day, pray for your needs, and ask him to bless the people you are close to.

Obedience

Consider the following questions:
- Is there any sin you have committed that you have trouble believing God has forgiven you? Declare Ephesians 1:7-8 and 1 John 1:9 over yourself and come into agreement with what God says about you.

- Do you find it hard to forgive someone? Make a list of names and events on a sheet of paper. Speak out loud that you forgive these people. Then pray for their well-being, that God would reach them and bless them. When you are done, rip up the paper and throw it away as a sign that you have totally forgiven them. Be sure to share your experience with your guide.

LESSON 6

Trusting God
Living by Faith

Faith: The Language of God

It has been said that faith is the language of God. Faith is what connects us to God; it is our "channel" of communication with the Holy Spirit who lives in us as Christ followers. There is no doubt that our relationship with God begins, grows, and matures through faith. We come to God in faith, believing that he is real and accessible to us.

And without faith it is impossible to please God, because anyone who comes to him must believe that he exists and that he rewards those who earnestly seek him. (Hebrews 11:6)

*But when you ask, you must **believe and not doubt**, because the one who doubts is like a wave of the sea, blown and tossed by the wind. 7That person should not expect to receive anything from the Lord. 8Such a person is double-minded and unstable in all they do.* (James 1:6-8)

When you speak to the Lord, you need to come in faith, truly believing that he hears you and will respond. Doubt can block your communication with God. You can be assured of God's love for you and that he will keep his word to you! Do not be double-minded. Go to God in faith, not doubt.

*It is important to understand that God does not respond to **need** as much as he responds to **faith**.* You can certainly bring your needs to God in prayer. In fact, we are told we should do that (Philippians 4:6). But when you come before God with your needs, do not beg him. This shows that you are not really sure that he will respond. You should ask in faith believing that God will answer your prayer. God responds to your faith in him to fulfill his promises!

God Is Always Good

You may think it is obvious that God is always good, but many times the thoughts and actions of Christians demonstrate they do not truly believe God is good in EVERY situation. We are like the disciples in the boat with Jesus when they encountered a sudden, strong storm, and Jesus remained sleeping! Here is the story in Mark.

> *37A furious squall came up, and the waves broke over the boat, so that it was nearly swamped. 38Jesus was in the stern, sleeping on a cushion. The disciples woke him and said to him, "Teacher, don't you care if we drown?" 39He got up, rebuked the wind and said to the waves, "Quiet! Be still!" Then the wind died down and it was completely calm. 40He said to his disciples, "Why are you so afraid? Do you still have no faith?" 41They were terrified and asked each other, "Who is this? Even the wind and the waves obey him!" (Mark 4:37-41)*

It is fascinating that the disciples became more terrified of Jesus than the storm! It is because they did not understand the magnitude of two things about Jesus – his love for them and his power. To the disciples at that time, Jesus was still the "teacher," but they found out he is much more! We fall into the same trap of not understanding that God is loving and good to us in EVERY situation. God is good ALWAYS, and he always has the power to rescue us. Jesus basically asked them, "Why are you so afraid? Don't you have faith that I am good and have the power to take care of you?" When you understand that God is always good and that he always loves you, you can live your life without fear.

> *There is no fear in love. But **perfect love drives out fear...***
> (1 John 4:18)

The truth is that if you do not believe God is always good, then you will come to believe you cannot always trust him. If you cannot trust him at all times, then you cannot put your total faith in him. Do not ever believe the lie that God is not always good! Do not agree with the accusations of the evil one that God is withholding something good from you, or that God does not really care for you, or that you are unworthy of God's love. God's love for you is unconditional. He has great things in store for you, and great plans for your life. You can trust him!

A New Reality: Walking By Faith, Not By Sight

For we live by faith, not by sight. (2 Corinthians 5:7)

*So we fix our eyes not on what is seen, but on what is unseen, since what is seen is temporary, but **what is unseen is eternal.*** (2 Corinthians 4:18)

Your journey with Jesus is a walk of faith. To be successful, you need to learn to *"see" things that are unseen* through a new spiritual lens. Although a challenge to comprehend at times, the spiritual world is the reality, while the natural world is just a manifestation of the spiritual realities around you. This does not mean that angels or demons are hiding behind every bush. It does mean you must ask God daily to help you discern the spiritual world and be led by the Holy Spirit.

It also means not everything in your walk with Jesus will make sense in the natural. Sometimes it is not easy to "see" what God is doing, but you can still trust him because he is always good. Stay near to Jesus and ask for the guidance of the Holy Spirit.

Sometimes the promises of God may be hard to "see" because they are delaying a long time. God gave Abraham a big promise that his descendants would form a nation, but having a child with his wife delayed for many years. In fact, his wife was past the age of having children. Look at how he stood in faith in the verses below:

*Yet he did not waver through unbelief regarding **the promise of God**, but was strengthened **in his faith** and gave glory to God, [21]being **fully persuaded** that God had power to do what he had promised.* (Romans 4:20-21)

Faith is being "fully persuaded" that God will keep his promises even though it does not look possible in the natural! That is how God wants us to live, and that kind of life is possible in Jesus. It is truly an adventure!

One final word about faith. Faith is not a feeling or only an inward conviction. True faith always requires a response on our part. We need to act on the word or promise that God has given us. You cannot have a "mailbox" mentality, sitting around doing nothing (or even praying) while you wait for the promise to just show up. The answer requires a "step of faith" on your part. If God tells you to walk on the water, you need to have the faith to step out of the boat!

A LOOK AT THE WORD

1. Read Hebrews 11:6.

   It is impossible to please God without what? Why? _____

   _____

   _____

   _____

2. Read James 1:6-8.

   What is a person like who doubts? _____

   _____

   _____

   Will they receive anything from the Lord? Why or why not?

   _____

   _____

3. Read Mark 4:37-41.

   What was Jesus doing when the storm came up on the lake and nearly filled the boat with water?_ _____

   Why did the disciples wake him up? _____

   _____

   How did Jesus respond to the storm and to the disciples?

   _____

   _____

   _____

4. Read 1 John 4:18.
   What does perfect love do? Why?

   _____

   _____

   _____

   _____

5. Read 2 Corinthians 5:7.
   How are we to live? _____

   _____

   _____

   Read 2 Corinthians 4:18.
   On what do we fix our eyes? Why? _____

   _____

   _____

6. Read Romans 4:20-21.
   How was Abraham's faith strengthened? _____

   _____

   _____

   _____

7. Read Hebrews 11:1.
   What is faith? _____

   _____

   _____

   _____

   Read Mark 11:22-24.
   In whom did Jesus say we are to have faith? Why? _____

   _____

   _____

   _____

APPLICATION

Faith grows in the soil of love. The more you understand God's unfailing love for you, the more faith you will have. God wants you to trust that he hears you and he has the power and desire to answer your prayers. When you doubt, James says that you are double-minded – you ask but are not sure if God will give it to you – and as a result you are unstable in all your ways. Unstable people question God's character and cannot be trusted. In Mark 4, the disciples doubted Jesus' love for them when they accused him of not caring if they drowned. Jesus' response was, in effect, "Why are you so afraid? Do you not have faith that I love you and will take care of you?"

When you understand God's love and that he is always with you, his perfect love should take away all fear. We fear because we do not believe God is with us, that he hears our prayers, or that he has the power and desire to answer. We also trust more in our natural senses (what we see, hear, smell, taste, and touch) than in what God actually says. It is time to believe like Abraham – fully persuaded that God has the power to do what he says. He does not lie; Satan does. It is time to stop believing the lies of our enemy and believe the One who loves us enough to die for us.

NEXT STEPS

Bible reading this week

Romans 11-16. Finish reading Romans this week. Romans is a letter written by the apostle Paul to the church in Rome. The focus is the righteousness of God and how God's grace is more powerful than sin.

Prayer

Pray for 10 minutes a day this week. Simply talk to God like you would a close friend. Thank him for your new life, ask him to lead you through the day, pray for your needs, and ask him to bless the people you are close to.

Obedience

Take a sheet of paper and fold it in half from top to bottom. On one side, write the lies you have believed about God (it could be things like he does not love you, has not forgiven a sin, does not heal, etc.) On the other side, write the truth from the Bible and write in the Scripture reference. Cut the paper in half. Rip up and throw away the side with the lies. Read out loud and declare the truth of God. Declare that God hears you, loves you, and will fulfill his promises!

You can make disciples in many nations!

If this book has been helpful to you, please consider helping it to be *printed and distributed in other nations of the world!*

Missio Global utilizes this book and the other books of the *Cross Series* for discipleship in several nations of the world. We currently want to add the following languages and nations:

- Portuguese in Brazil
- Swahili in Tanzania and East Africa
- Ukrainian in Ukraine

It typically costs about $2.50 per copy to print a book. At this rate, **a $100 contribution will print 40 copies of a book.** That is a tremendous investment in discipling the nations!

Please consider helping to GO and make disciples in the nations. Your tax deductible donation *(designate for Translation Fund)* can be made online at:

www.missioglobal.org

or sent by check to:

Missio Global
PO Box 17211
Asheville, NC 28816

THANK YOU!

Answers

Lesson 1 – Becoming a Disciple

1. Mark 3:14-15
   - Jesus appointed the 12 disciples so they might be with him and that he might send them out to preach and have authority to drive out demons.
   - It is important to be with Jesus so that I can learn to be more like him and to do the works he did (add any other answers you think are important).
   - I do this by reading the Bible, praying, listening, giving, serving, and spending time with others that know him (like at church, a small group, or discipleship relationship).

2. Matthew 10:24-25
   - The goal of a student in is to be like his teacher.
   - Some teachers in my life are…(pastor, small group leader, someone discipling you, Bible teacher on radio, TV, or internet, etc.).

3. Matthew 11:28-30
   - A yoke is put around the neck of farm animals to plow a field or pull a cart. When two animals are used, it lessens the burden of weight each must pull.
   - The yoke of Jesus is easy and his burden is light because he is pulling most, if not all, of the weight.
   - If I feel as though the yoke of Jesus is heavy, it may be because I am pulling most of the weight; I am carrying most of the burden. (Add any other reasons you may have.)

4. John 14:12-14
   - We will be able to do greater things than Jesus because he has gone to be with the Father (he is now with the Father).
   - We do that by asking for anything in Jesus' name because the Father is glorified in the Son.

5. Matthew 28:18-20
   - Making disciples was Jesus' priority because he wanted everyone to know about him and find forgiveness, love,

healing, rest, etc.

Lesson 2 – Making Jesus Lord

1. Romans 10:9-10
    - To be saved you must **declare** with your mouth 'Jesus is Lord,' and **believe** in your heart that God raised him from the dead.

    - You must do both because when you **believe** with your heart you are **justified** (declared right or innocent) and when you **declare** your faith with your mouth you are **saved**.

2. Luke 9:23-25
    - To be a disciple of Jesus you must take up your cross daily and follow him.

    - This means that to follow Jesus means you must die to yourself and do what Jesus teaches us to do in his Word.

    - You do this because if you want to save your life you must lose it, but if you lose your life you will save it. You can gain the whole world (riches, homes, etc.) but lose eternal life.

3. Luke 14:27 and 33
    - To be a disciple of Jesus you must carry your cross – be willing to give up everything.

    - God is asking me to give up…….(examples: something you do like drinking, smoking, sex before marriage, gossiping; something you have like types of clothing; someone you like, or perhaps God wants you to forgive someone who hurt you.)

4. Mark 10:17-22
    - The man asked Jesus, "what must I do to inherit eternal life?"

    - He had kept the commandments listed by Jesus.

    - Jesus said he needed to sell everything, give to the poor, and then follow him

    - The man went away sad because he had great wealth and found this hard to give up.

5. 1 Corinthians 13:3
    - Giving to the poor or living in hardship is not necessarily evidence that Jesus is Lord of your heart. These good works should be an outflow of your love for Jesus.

Lesson 3 – Obedience: The Law vs. The Heart

1. Matthew 5:21-22
    - Jesus considers being angry with a brother or sister to also be murder.

    - Murdering someone and being angry were both considered to be murder and therefore subject to judgement.

    Matthew 5:27-28
    - Jesus considers looking lustfully at a woman adultery because the person has committed adultery in his heart.

2. John 14:15 – You show your love for Jesus by keeping his commands.

3. John 14:23-24
    - You can know those who love Jesus because they obey his teachings; those who do not love him do not obey his teachings.

    - The reward for obedience is that the Father will love the person and Jesus and the Father will make their home with him.

4. Luke 11:28
    - Jesus says those who hear God's word and obey it are blessed.

    - If I hear and follow his commands I will be blessed.

5. 2 John 1:6 – I walk in love when I obey God's commands.

Lesson 4 – Sanctification: Becoming More Like Jesus

1. Hebrews 10:14
    - Jesus' sacrifice on the cross made us perfect.

    - We were *made* "perfect" the moment we believed in Jesus and declared him Lord because our sins were completely forgiven. We are *being made* holy (becoming more like Christ) as we choose to obey and walk with God. Being made perfect is a process for the rest of our lives.

2. Romans 6:19b-22
   - I offered myself as a slave to impurity and to ever-increasing wickedness.
   - When I was a slave to sin I was free from the control of righteousness.
   - The result was death.
   - Now I am a slave to God.
   - I am set free from sin.
   - The result is eternal life.

3. Hebrews 12:1-2a
   - I am to throw off everything that hinders and the sin that entangles my ability to run.
   - I am to run the race marked out for me with perseverance.
   - According to this verse Jesus is the pioneer (author) and "perfecter" of my faith.
   - The race marked out for me now is… (put in what you sense or believe is God's purpose for you).

4. 1 Timothy 4:7-8
   - Physical training has some value: it keeps your body healthy, helps you maintain good weight, strengthens your muscles, keeps your heart strong.
   - Training yourself to be godly has more value because it has value for all things in the present life and in the life to come.
   - Things I can do to train myself to be godly: Seek God daily through prayer and Bible reading, give tithes and offerings, serve others, gather regularly with other believers (at church, small group, prayer groups, etc.), listen to teachings, read books, confess my sins to others, allow others to correct me, asking forgiveness for sins, forgiving others, etc.

Lesson 5 – Forgiveness: Receiving and Giving

1. 1 John 1:9 – God is faithful and just to cleanse us from unrighteousness.

2. Ephesians 1:7-8
   - Redemption is the act of buying something back.

- We have redemption and forgiveness of sins according to the riches of God's grace.
- Lavish means to give an abundance, an excessive amount. We are given an excessive amount of God's grace.

3. Matthew 18:21-35
   - We are to forgive 70 times 7. Jesus was not placing a limit but was saying you must always forgive.
   - The first man owes 10,000 bags of gold (In Greek it says 10,000 talents, which about 20 years of a day laborer's wage).
   - To pay the debt his wife and children were to be sold.
   - The master forgave the whole debt when the servant begged for the master to be patient.
   - The second man owed his fellow servant 100 silver coins (In Greek it says 100 denarii; a denarius was the usual daily wage of a day laborer).
   - When the second man asked for mercy his fellow servant refused and had the man thrown in prison.
   - Even if the servant had received his money it would not have been enough to pay off his debt to the master.
   - The master called the servant wicked because he refused to forgive the debt. He handed him over to the jailers to be tortured until he could pay back all he owed.
   - The debt I owe to Jesus is huge, too big for me to ever pay back. Jesus was teaching that our debt is too big for us to pay, like the first servant, and God forgave us. Therefore, we must always forgive those who sin against us no matter how big or small the debt.

4. Matthew 6:14-15
   - It is important to forgive others when they sin against me because my heavenly Father will forgive me when I sin. If I don't forgive others, he will not forgive me.
   - Forgiving others delivers us from the evil one because it keeps us from bitterness and hurt that are the result of holding an offense. Forgiveness will also keep us from pride, thinking that somehow we are less sinful than someone else.

Lesson 6 – Trusting God: Living by Faith

1. Hebrews 11:6 – It is impossible to please God without faith because you must believe that he exists and that he rewards those who seek him.

2. James 1:6-8
    *   A person who doubts is like a wave of the sea that is blown and tossed by the wind.
    *   They will not receive anything from the Lord because they are double-minded and unstable in all they do.

3. Mark 4:37-41
    *   When the storm came up on the lake Jesus was sleeping on a cushion in the stern.
    *   The disciples woke him up because they were afraid they would drown and accused him of not caring.
    *   Jesus calmed the storm and then asked the disciples why they were so afraid and if they still had no faith.

4. 1 John 4:18 – Perfect love casts out fear. It does this because perfect love is God, and if he is with us we do not need to fear.

5. 2 Corinthians 5:7 – We are to live by faith and not by sight.

    2 Corinthians 4:18 – This means that we fix our eyes on what is unseen because it is eternal, rather than on what is seen because it is temporary.

6. Romans 4:20-21 –Abraham was strengthened in his faith about the promise of God, because he was fully persuaded that God had power to do what he had promised.

7. Hebrews 11:1 – Faith is being confident in what we hope for and sure about what we do not see.

    Mark 11:22-24 – Jesus tells us to have faith in God because whatever we ask for in prayer, if we believe we have received it, it will be ours (even something as big as telling a mountain to go throw itself into the sea).

THE CROSS SERIES

The Cross Series is a book series for Christian growth focusing on discipleship and the initial stages of leadership development. The material is best used in one-on-one mentorship relationships or in small groups. The Cross Series is designed as a growth track that leads to the church-based Missio Global School of Ministry. It can also be used as valuable equipping material for general Christian discipleship. Titles include:

CrossWalk – *First Steps in Your Walk with God*

CrossFire – *A New Way of Living (Books 1 & 2)*

Project 2T2:2
Making Disciple Makers!

Complete the three books of **The Cross Series** (*CrossWalk* and *CrossFire - Books 1 &2*) and then help guide another person through the books! *Be a disciple maker and help change the world!*

Project 2 Timothy 2:2
And the things you have heard me say in the presence of many witnesses entrust to reliable people who will also be qualified to teach others.

Missio Global School of Ministry

This material is used in conjunction with the Missio Global School of Ministry, a partnership between Missio Global and churches around the world. The School is a valuable one or three-year training program that is based in the local church. It is a proven tool that churches can use to equip their congregation and develop emerging leaders.

For information on hosting a School of Ministry in your church, contact us at: **www.missioglobal.org**.

Missio Global School of Ministry

This material is used in conjunction with the Missio Global School of Ministry, a partnership between Missio Global and churches around the world. The School is a valuable tool for those containing a program that is used to train churches. It is a proven tool that churches use to fully equip their congregation and develop competent leaders.

For information on hosting a School of Ministry in your church, contact us at www.missioglobal.com